## Lives and Times
# Wolfgang Amadeus Mozart

Peggy Pancella

Heinemann Library
Chicago, Illinois

Designed by Lucy Owen and Bridge Creative Services
Originated by Modern Age Repro
Printed and bound by South China Printing Company

10 09 08 07 06
10 9 8 7 6 5 4 3 2 1

**Library of Congress Cataloging-in-Publication Data**
Pancella, Peggy.
  Wolfgang Amadeus Mozart / Peggy Pancella.
    p. cm. -- (Lives and times)
  Includes bibliographical references and index.
  ISBN 1-4034-6747-1 (library binding-hardcover)
  1. Mozart, Wolfgang Amadeus, 1756-1791--Juvenile
literature. 2. Composers--Austria--Biography--Juvenile
literature. I. Title. II. Series: Lives and times (Des
Plaines, Ill.)
  ML3930.M9P36 2005
  780'.92--dc22
                                    2005001500

**Acknowledgments**
The author and publishers are grateful to the following
for permission to reproduce copyright material:
AKG-Images pp. **7**, **12**; AKG-Images/Erich Lessing p. **9**;
AKG-Images/Mozart-Mus.d.Stift.Mozarteum, Salzburg
p. **18**; AKG-Images/Staatsbibl. Preuß.Kulturbesitz p. **5**;
Alamy/Alan Copson p. **26**; Alamy/Jenny Andre p. **19**;
Alamy/Jon Arnold Images p. **6**; Alamy/Popperfoto p. **16**;
Corbis/Archivo Iconografico, S.A. pp. **4**, **24**;
Corbis/Bettmann p. **14**; Corbis/Robbie Jack p. **17**;
Corbis/The State Hermitage Museum, St. Petersburg,
Russia p. **11**; Kathryn Prewitt p. **8**, **15**, **22**; The
Bridgeman Art Library/Gavin Graham Gallery p. **20**;
The Bridgeman Art Library/Haags Gemeentemuseum,
The Hague, Netherlands p. **10**; The Bridgeman Art
Library/Hunterian Art Gallery p. **21**; The Bridgeman
Art Library/Mozart Museum, Salzburg, Austria pp. **13**,
**23**; The Bridgeman Art Library/Private Collection p. **25**;
The Kobal Collection/Saul Zaentz Company p. **27**.

Cover picture of Wolfgang Amadeus Mozart
reproduced with permission of Getty News & Sport.
Photograph of music manuscript reproduced with
permission of Corbis.

Page icons by Digital Vision

Photo research by Maria Joannou and Virginia
Stroud-Lewis

Every effort has been made to contact copyright
holders of any material reproduced in this book.
Any omissions will be rectified in subsequent
printings if notice is given to the publishers.

# Contents

Some words are shown in bold, **like this**. You can find out what they mean by looking in the glossary.

# Introducing Wolfgang Amadeus Mozart

Wolfgang Amadeus Mozart was very good at music. As a child he learned to play several instruments. He performed all over Europe. People were amazed that he could play so well.

Wolfgang wrote more than 600 pieces of music in his short life.

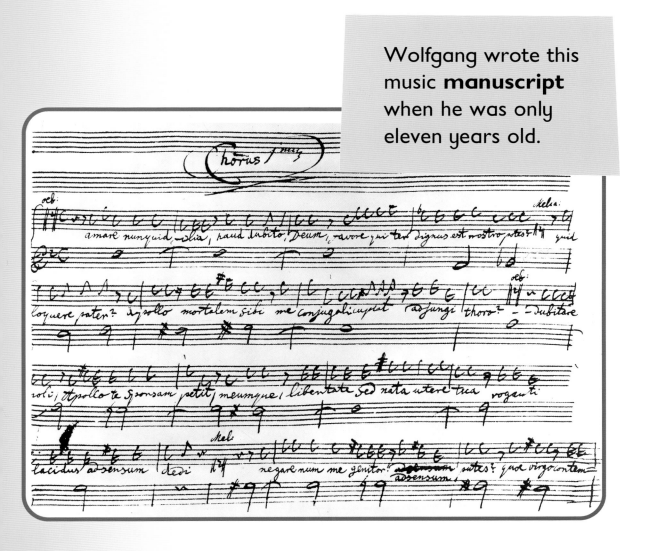

Wolfgang wrote this music **manuscript** when he was only eleven years old.

Wolfgang also wrote his own music. His music was very popular. Some people think he was the greatest **composer** ever.

# Little Wolfie

Wolfgang was born in Austria on January 27, 1756. He was the last of seven children. Only he and his older sister, Nannerl, lived past childhood. His family called him "Wolferl" or "Wolfie."

The house where Wolfgang was born is now a museum.

Wolfgang's father, Leopold, was a **musician**. He taught Nannerl to play the **clavier**. Wolfgang wanted to learn, too. At first he tried only a few notes.

Wolfgang was three when he first tried the clavier. He could barely reach the keys.

# Early Learning

Wolfgang never went to school. Instead his father taught him at home. He studied many subjects, but he loved music best. He spent hours at the **keyboard**.

Sometimes Wolfgang wrote his math problems on a blackboard in his house.

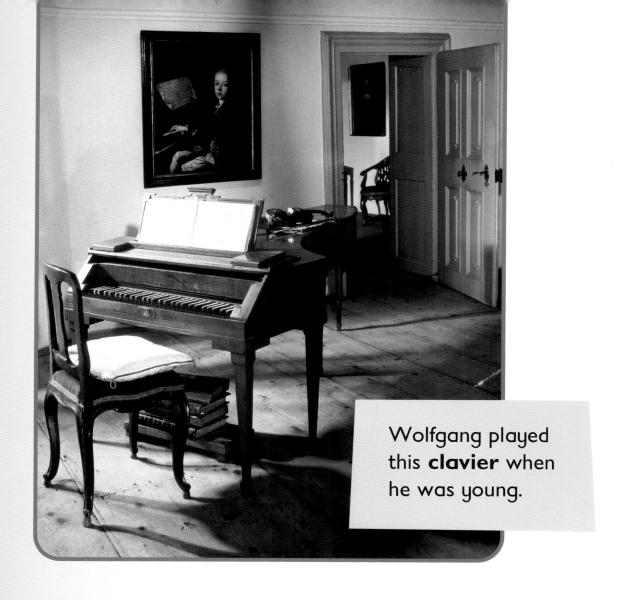

Wolfgang played this **clavier** when he was young.

Wolfgang learned very quickly. At four he could play all the pieces in Nannerl's music book. Then he **composed** his own pieces and learned to write them down.

# Musical Talent

People soon realized that Wolfgang had special **talents**. He played new tunes perfectly on the first try. He **composed** music, and played the **clavier** as well as an adult. And he was only five years old!

Wolfgang often practiced music with his father and his sister.

Once Wolfgang's father was playing music with friends. They let Wolfgang play along quietly with a violin. Soon they stopped in amazement. Wolfgang had taught himself to play the violin!

Wolfgang's violin music was beautiful. He did not need any lessons.

# Playing at the Palace

Wolfgang's father was proud of his children. He hoped that their music might make the family rich and famous. So he took the children on long **tours** through Europe. They played for many important people.

Wolfgang was six the first time he played in Vienna. Nannerl was eleven.

The empress gave Wolfgang fine clothes as a gift. He was very proud of them.

On one trip the family went to Austria's **capital city**, Vienna. They played for the royal family. **Empress** Maria Theresa loved their music.

# Life on Tour

The Mozarts spent several years on **tour** in Europe. They became more and more famous. People gave them money and gifts. They loved the attention and the nice things people said.

Wolfgang was very good at playing the **organ**. People who heard him were amazed.

Touring was not always easy, though. The roads were bad, so travel was slow. Wolfgang was often very sick. Sometimes Papa and Nannerl were ill, too. Finally, the family returned home.

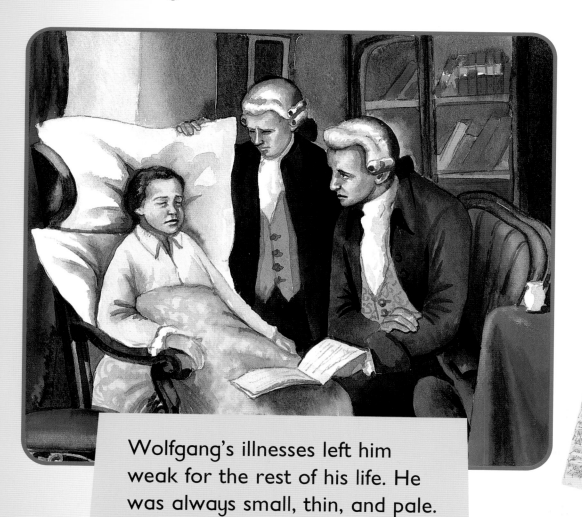

Wolfgang's illnesses left him weak for the rest of his life. He was always small, thin, and pale.

# Work and Play

Wolfgang's head was full of ideas for new music. He **composed** his first **symphony** for an **orchestra** at age eight. At twelve he wrote his first **opera**. He often worked day and night until a piece was finished.

This is a picture of Mozart at the age of twelve.

Today orchestras and singers often perform Wolfgang's music. This is a scene from his opera, *The Magic Flute*.

Wolfgang also found time for fun. He enjoyed playing cards and billiards, a game like pool. He loved to write letters, too. His letters were full of jokes, rhymes, and even secret codes.

# Growing Up

Wolfgang left home to find work when he was 21 years old. But he had more fun going to parties. He also fell in love with a girl named Aloysia. Wolfgang's father told him to forget about Aloysia and get a job.

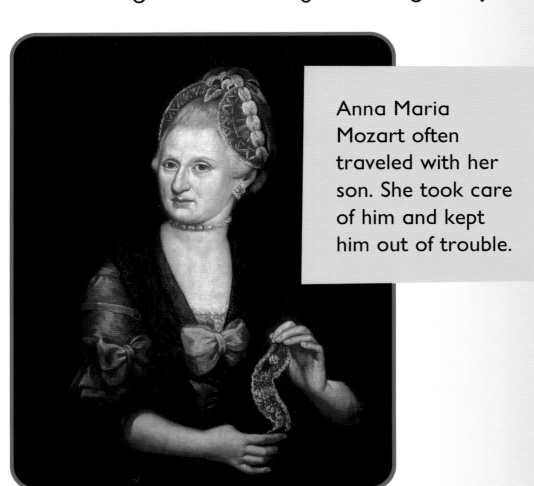

Anna Maria Mozart often traveled with her son. She took care of him and kept him out of trouble.

Wolfgang found work at this palace in Paris, but he chose not to take the job.

Wolfgang and his mother went to Paris, France. But they did not like the people or the weather. Wolfgang's mother became ill and soon died. Before long he sadly returned home to his father.

# A New Start

Back at home Wolfgang played the **organ** and wrote church music. He also **composed** an **opera**. But his boss treated him like a servant. After a huge argument, Wolfgang quit.

This is Wolfgang's hometown of Salzburg, Austria.

Wolfgang did not have a job, but he was happy to be free. He was also in love again. He wanted to marry Aloysia's sister, Constanze. His father did not like the idea, but Wolfgang ignored him.

Constanze was a fine singer. Wolfgang married her in 1782.

# A Fine Life

Wolfgang and Constanze were very happy. They had a fine home and fancy clothes. They held many grand parties. Soon they had two sons. Wolfgang was spending a lot of money.

The Mozarts had their own carriage, even though it cost a lot of money.

Wolfgang and Constanze had six children, but only two sons survived. They were called Franz and Karl.

Sometimes they spent too much money. Wolfgang gave concerts, taught lessons, and **composed** new music to earn more money. In hard times the family burned furniture in the fireplace to keep warm.

# The End Nears

Wolfgang went to work for **Emperor** Joseph II in 1787. He **composed** a lot of new music. Some of his **operas** became very popular. But soon Wolfgang grew ill.

This painting of Wolfgang was made towards the end of his life.

Wolfgang's friends visited him the day before he died. They sang parts of his *Requiem* together.

A stranger asked Wolfgang to write a **requiem**. Wolfgang agreed, but he was very weak. He could not finish the piece. Wolfgang died on December 5, 1791. He was only 35 years old.

# The Music Goes On

Wolfgang's family did not have much money. They gave him a very simple funeral. No one even knows where he is buried. But people will never forget his beautiful music.

There are many statues of Wolfgang in Europe. This one is in Vienna.

Amadeus is a movie about Wolfgang's life. It helped get people interested in his music.

**Musicians** still perform Wolfgang's music today. **Choirs** around the world sang his **Requiem** on September 11, 2002. They honored those who had died one year earlier in attacks on the United States.

# Fact File

- People sometimes covered young Wolfgang's hands with a cloth while he played music. But this did not bother him. He could play well without seeing the keys.

- When Wolfgang was fourteen, he listened to a **choir** singing a famous song. He remembered the music in his head. Later he wrote down every single note from memory.

- Wolfgang became friends with another great **composer** named Franz Joseph Haydn. They liked to play music together. Wolfgang wrote several pieces of music for his friend.

- Many composers were good at just one kind of music. Some wrote **operas** well. Some were better at writing **symphonies**. Others wrote music for church services. But Wolfgang was good at writing all different kinds of music.

# Timeline

| | |
|---|---|
| **1756** | Wolfgang is born in Austria, on January 27 |
| **1759** | Wolfgang begins learning to play the **clavier** |
| **1760** | Wolfgang **composes** his first music |
| **1762** | Wolfgang's first **tour**; he plays for **Empress** Maria Theresa in Vienna |
| **1764** | Wolfgang writes his first **symphony** |
| **1768** | Wolfgang composes his first **opera** |
| **1777** | Wolfgang tours without his father for the first time; he falls in love with Aloysia |
| **1778** | Wolfgang and his mother travel to Paris; she becomes ill and dies there |
| **1779** | Wolfgang returns home |
| **1782** | Wolfgang marries Constanze |
| **1784** | Wolfgang's son Karl is born |
| **1787** | Wolfgang's father dies; Wolfgang starts working for **Emperor** Joseph II |
| **1791** | Wolfgang's son Franz is born; Wolfgang dies on December 5 |

# Glossary

**capital city** main city where the people in charge of a state or country live and work

**choir** group of singers

**clavier** early type of keyboard instrument

**compose** to make up music

**composer** person who makes up music

**emperor** person who rules a large land or group of lands

**empress** wife of an emperor or a woman who rules a large land or group of lands by herself

**keyboard** row or set of keys that can be pressed to make sound

**manuscript** anything written by hand

**musician** person who makes music

**opera** play with words that are sung, not spoken

**orchestra** musical group that contains different instruments

**organ** keyboard instrument that makes many different sounds, usually by pushing air through pipes

**requiem** music written in honor of someone who has died

**symphony** long piece of music written for many musical instruments to play together

**talent** special gift or ability to do something

**tour** long trip with stops at different places

# Find Out More

## More Books to Read

Cencetti, Greta. *Mozart*. New York, N.Y.: Peter Bedrick Books, 2001.

Costanza, Stephen. *Mozart Finds a Melody*. New York, N.Y.: Henry Holt & Co., 2004.

Turner, Barrie Carson. *Wolfgang Amadeus Mozart*. North Mankato, Minn.: Chrysalis Education, 2003.

## Places to Visit

There are many places that honor Wolfgang today. These include:

Wolfgang's birthplace, Salzburg, Austria
Mozart Museum, Vienna, Austria.

In the United States, many places have festivals of Wolfgang's music. These include:

New York City, New York (Lincoln Center for the Performing Arts)
San Francisco, California
Burlington, Vermont
San Diego, California
San Luis Obispo, California.

# Index